Contents

Meet the sheep

Baa! Sheep graze in the sun on the farm. The flock's hard hooves sink into the soft ground.

4

Sheep have thick fur
called wool. A sheep's
wool can be white, tan,
brown or other colours.
Some sheep are spotted.

About 900 different breeds of sheep live around the world. An adult sheep can weigh up to 181 kilograms (400 pounds), depending on its breed.

Adults and babies

Male and female sheep live
on the farm. Males are called
rams. Female sheep are
called ewes. Rams and ewes
live for 6 to 11 years.

ewe

A baby sheep is called a lamb.

Lambs are born in spring.

They can stand soon after birth.

Lambs jump and play together.

Time to eat

Sheep eat grass and plants.

They also eat hay and grain.

Sheep swallow their food.

Then later they burp up the

food and chew it.

On the farm

Farmers keep sheep for their meat and wool. Sometimes sheep are kept for their milk. A sheep's wool is made into clothing and blankets.

wool

Farmers shave the sheep's
wool in late spring or early
summer. This is called shearing.
The wool can weigh up to
9 kilograms (20 pounds) each year.

Foxes and other predators attack sheep. Farmers use dogs, donkeys and llamas to watch over flocks. Sheep stay safe on the farm.

Glossary

breed   particular kind of animal within an animal group

flock   group of animals that lives or moves together; a group of sheep is called a flock

graze   eat grass that is growing in a field

hoof   hard covering over the foot of some types of animal; sheep, horses and deer have hooves

pasture   land where farm animals eat grass and exercise

predator   animal that hunts other animals for food

wool   soft, thick, curly hair of sheep and some other animals, such as llamas and alpacas

Read more

Animals on the Farm (Animals I Can See), Sian Smith (Raintree, 2015)

Farm Animals (Tadpole Learners), Annabelle Lynch (Franklin Watts, 2015)

Farm Animals: True or False? (True or False?), Daniel Nunn (Raintree, 2013)

Websites

www.dkfindout.com/uk/animals-and-nature/domesticated-animals/sheep
Learn more about sheep and see a diagram of what they look like.

www.sciencekids.co.nz/sciencefacts/animals/sheep.html
Read fun facts about sheep.

Index